KV-428-430

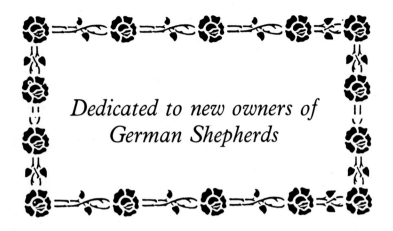

Dedicated to new owners of German Shepherds

Front endpapers: A trio of German Shepherds worthy of representing the breed.

Back endpapers: A German Shepherd bred and trained for conformation is easy to recognize.

Title page: Head of a typical German Shepherd.

A Beginner's Guide to
German Shepherds

Written By
Franklin Steinitz

Contents

© 1986 by T.F.H. Publications, Inc. Distributed in the UNITED STATES by T.F.H. Publications, Inc., 211 West Sylvania Avenue, Neptune City, NJ 07753; in CANADA by H & L Pet Supplies Inc., 27 Kingston Crescent, Kitchener, Ontario N2B 2T6; Rolf C. Hagen Ltd., 3225 Sartelon Street, Montreal 382 Quebec; in CANADA to the Book Trade by Macmillan of Canada (A Division of Canada Publishing Corporation), 164 Commander Boulevard, Agincourt, Ontario M1S 3C7; in ENGLAND by T.F.H. Publications Limited, 4 Kier Park, Ascot, Berkshire SL5 7DS; in AUSTRALIA AND THE SOUTH PACIFIC by T.F.H. (Australia) Pty. Ltd., Box 149, Brookvale 2100 N.S.W., Australia; in NEW ZEALAND by Ross Haines & Son, Ltd., 18 Monmouth Street, Grey Lynn, Auckland 2 New Zealand; in SINGAPORE AND MALAYSIA by MPH Distributors (S) Pte., Ltd., 601 Sims Drive, #03/07/21, Singapore 1438; in the PHILIPPINES by Bio-Research, 5 Lippay Street, San Lorenzo Village, Makati Rizal; in SOUTH AFRICA by Multipet Pty. Ltd., 30 Turners Avenue, Durban 4001. Published by T.F.H. Publications, Inc. Manufactured in the United States of America by T.F.H. Publications, Inc.

1.
History

In selecting a German Shepherd you have chosen one of the most intelligent and useful members of the whole family of dogs. These handsome animals were originally bred as work-dogs; they tended herds of sheep in Central Europe. Today they are also highly prized for their

The German Shepherd is called by some other names, like the Alsatian and Police Dog, in English-speaking countries. Photo by A. Wintzell.

Originally bred as working dogs for the farm, German Shepherds are now in great demand for guard work in many of the urban areas of the world.

beauty, companionship, and alertness. In addition, owners of German Shepherds soon learn to appreciate the intelligence and utility for which the breed was first developed.

Closely identified as a "Seeing-Eye" dog, the German Shepherd is trained for police and military work as well. His war-time citations are numerous. In peaceful pursuits, he's known as a dog who can think and act on his own to prevent a child from being hurt or to save someone in distress.

A well trained German Shepherd can provide protection to your property and family from unwanted intruders. Photo by Sally Anne Thompson.

A most welome dip in the family swimming pool. Photo by Sally Anne Thompson.

Yes, there is no doubt that his quiet dignity and handsome form provide great pride of ownership. Some of us may remember the old silent film days of Rin-Tin-Tin as our first recognition of the German Shepherd. Today, the German Shepherd remains the standard to which other dogs are compared.

Centuries ago

Centuries ago in Europe, sheep raising was much more important than it is today, and consequently sheep dogs were widely bred. In the mountainous area of Southern Europe, large husky dogs developed that could climb steep hills to guard the herds. In the flat plains area of Northern Europe the herds moved farther and faster. Here a smaller, thinner dog evolved, one that could cover long distances without tiring. There were, too, many in-between sizes, colors and types of sheep dogs.

Only selective breeding from parents with characteristics that come close to the requirements of the Standard can produce a magnificent German Shepherd.

Max von Stephanitz, a German cavalry captain, became very interested in these dogs toward the end of the last century. In 1889 he established the *Verein für Deutsche Schaferhunde,* which in English means the Club for German Shepherd Dogs. Von Stephanitz and his club set standards for the breed in Germany and enforced them ruthlessly. Dogs had to be bred for intelligence and utility; beauty was only a by-product. Today leadership in breeding German Shepherds has passed to the United States and standards have changed somewhat over the years. However, it is still their intelligence and willingness to serve man as well as their natural beauty that makes them loved in so many countries.

Improvements in breeding

The original breeders in Germany, as well as the modern ones throughout the world, set "standards" or ideal characteristics for the dogs they bred. The standards followed by breeders today are those adopted by the

Two show dogs having fun with the family kids. Photo by Sally Anne Thompson.

Learning to scale a high wall is a prerequisite for a German Shepherd intended to perform police work. Photo by Sally Anne Thompson.

German Shepherd Dog Club of America. These standards have changed only slightly over the years, and these basic characteristics have made the German Shepherd of today truly a magnificent animal.

The first impression of a good German Shepherd is that of a strong, agile, well-muscled animal, alert and full of life. He is well balanced and well developed, and slightly longer than he is tall. The good German Shepherd male is about 25 inches high at the shoulder and the female is slightly smaller. They usually weigh between 60 and 85 pounds. In recent years there has been a tendency to breed bulkier and taller dogs. It is not uncommon to see males 28 inches high and weighing well over 100 pounds.

His head is clean-cut and strong and gives him a look of quality and nobility. His muzzle is long and strong and his forehead is slightly arched, not rounded or domed. The ears are moderately pointed and open toward the front. His eyes are medium-sized and show a keen, intelligent look.

He has strong, white teeth, and when he bites they meet with a slight overbite.

His body gives an impression of depth and solidity without being too bulky. His chest is deep and comes forward off his shoulders. His abdomen is firm and does not hang too low. He is a large dog, though, and his abdomen will never come up as high as a Greyhound's or that of other racing dogs. He is slightly longer than he is high, in the proportion of 10 to 8½ inches.

His legs are reasonably straight and in proportion to his overall size. He has short, compact feet with well-arched toes, pads that are thick and hard, and nails short and strong. The hind legs which are characteristic of the breed should be distinctly angulated or set back at an angle. They are a little long so that he runs at a characteristic "stride," reaching forward with them as he runs. This contributes to a smooth tireless gait. When a German Shepherd runs, his back should remain level, almost seeming to float along in contrast to other dogs, whose backs bob up and down.

Of all the attributes of the fine German Shepherd, perhaps the most valuable is his good character. He has a quiet confidence that shows he is willing to serve his master in any capacity that circumstances may require. He is never timid, nor is he a nervous "fear biter," snapping at strangers merely because he is confused or apprehensive.

2.
Selecting

Choosing a German Shepherd puppy is a lot of fun. You naturally want one who seems to like you, and how nice it is to have a little puppy who seems to have picked *you* out for his own! At the same time, you look for those

The Floppy ears of this German Shepherd puppy will stand erect gradually as he gets older. Cropping the ears is not necessary. Photo by Fritz Prenzel.

features that tell you that he will grow up to be a healthy, handsome companion.

First, compare the size of all the pups in the litter. One dog may be much larger than the others, and there may be a runt in the litter. Your dog is neither of these, since it is the average-looking puppy who usually grows up to be the best-looking dog.

Since you want a dog that will be alert and enjoy life, you look for signs of good health. Your puppy is cute and floppy, of course, but he is also awake and curious, trying to explore his little world. He has straight legs (as straight as a little puppy's can be), and his bones and feet are large and out of proportion to his size. In fact, he will sometimes appear to be "all feet". As his body size increases and he puts on weight, he becomes a well-balanced dog.

Look at his head carefully. It is already rather long, though not, of course, as long as when he is full grown. His eyes are dark and alert-looking. His teeth meet well, with the upper front teeth closing slightly over the lowers. The ears may still be floppy, as these frequently do not stand up until the pup is three to six months old.

There is no need to look for the finer points of beauty in your puppy while he is so young. Since he is healthy and reasonably well-built, you just have to wait for about six months, then you can decide about entering him in dog shows. Even if he turns out to have a tail that's a little too long or an ear that insists on flopping over, you will still have a wonderful friend and wouldn't trade him for all the blue-ribbon show dogs in the world.

3.
Housing

Don't expect your new German Shepherd puppy to settle down and make himself at home like an old-timer. After all, he's just a little puppy and the world is still strange to him. This is probably the first time he has been away from his family. He is a little nervous and a

Experienced dog breeders state that puppies between the age of eight to twelve weeks generally adjust well to their new owners.

little afraid of his new home. He may cry often during the first few days. He may even be noisy all night long.

First few nights

For those first few nights you and your family are the substitutes for his family. Keep him nice and warm by putting him near a warm radiator, under an infrared warming lamp, next to a wrapped-up hot water bottle, but not in your own bed unless you intend to keep him as a bed mate.

After a few days he will become accustomed to all the smells and sounds of his new home. He will then realize you and your family are his best friends and will settle down.

A light chain choke collar or any other type of a light collar and a leash are basic equipment for a new dog. Photo by Sally Anne Thompson.

Consider carefully the diet and feeding schedule of your German Shepherd. Photo by Sally Anne Thompson.

Puppy's new bed

You may keep your German Shepherd pup indoors or out. In either case, he must have his own bed. If he is kept indoors, pick a sleeping area for him as you would for yourself. It should be warm and quiet so that he will get his proper sleep. His bed may be purchased at your local pet shop. It should be kept in the same place so that your pup can depend on a quiet familiar place to get his needed sleep.

If he is to live outdoors, you must provide a doghouse for him. This may be very simple or very fancy, depending on your taste. When you buy his house, remember that he will soon be a very large dog and will need lots of room. His house should have some standing room, about three feet high. Floor space should be about three feet by five feet. If you can spare the extra expense, you might provide his house with a covered porch on the front. He can lie there in rainy weather and keep an eye on things in general. Hang a heavy curtain over the front door during cold weather.

A magnificent head study of a typical German Shepherd. Note his dark eyes and black nose.

4.
Caring

Use common sense

There are a great many methods of feeding, housebreaking, and grooming German Shepherds. Actually, German Shepherds are like people, in that no two are alike.

Proper brushing is a pleasurable experience. Your Shepherd should not fret when brushed. Photo by Sally Anne Thompson.

You soon learn that your dog is an individual and you must do what is best for him, not what is best for other dogs. In using the advice given here on caring for him, remember that a little common sense will substitute for a lot of experience.

Your German Shepherd has been bred for intelligence as well as for his other desirable traits. You will want to take advantage of his great intelligence in caring for him. Let his actions be guides for you. For example, a certain amount of food might be recommended. If he is healthy and is content with less, you should cut the amount of food. If he complains when you brush his right shoulder, he is asking you to investigate because there is something wrong with his shoulder.

Use your common sense and treat him as an intelligent individual and you and your Shepherd friend will be able to handle any feeding and grooming problems that may arise.

Mealtime

Your German Shepherd thrives on meat just as the wolf does, but this does not mean that he can be a healthy dog eating only lean red meat. He needs many food components that are not found in lean red meat. The wolf gets them by eating practically all the parts of animals he catches. Your dog must get them in the balanced diet you provide. There are many such diets possible today with the veterinary vitamin and mineral supplements, protein-rich treats, etc.

The puppy lives only on his mother's milk for the first seventeen or eighteen days. By that time his teeth are beginning to appear and he can be fed other foods. Ask

A German Shepherd bitch from the Duranburg Shepherd Kennel in California. Photo by Louise van der Meid.

The ability to discriminate scents is indispensable for advance obedience training, police work, and leading the blind. Photo by Sally Anne Thompson.

your veterinarian or pet shop owner for advice on feeding your dog, as they will know best.

After your puppy is four months old, you should feed him only three times a day and give him a little more for each meal, the diet recommended by your vet or pet shop owner. You may wish to try a meal of dry food. If you use dry meal mixed with milk or water add a little fat and scraps. Give him some boiled milk before bedtime.

When he becomes six months old you may start feeding him only twice a day. Give him about two cups of food in the morning and about three cups in the evening. These amounts are approximate. If he wants more let him have all he wants; there'll be time enough to diet when he's an adult.

A commercially prepared veterinary vitamin and mineral powder should be included with the dog's food, following the directions on the package. It is a good idea also for growth and coat to add recommended amounts of a commercially prepared cod-liver oil and wheat germ oil several times weekly.

After his first birthday you may feed him only one large meal each day if you and the dog agree on it. If he obviously prefers two meals a day then divide it in two. Watch his eating habits and adjust his meals as you do your own. If he doesn't eat all of his food, cut down on the size of the meals. If he needs to put on weight, add more fat to the diet. Scraps from your own table are good for him for variety, but be careful NEVER to give him fish or poultry bones. It's a good policy to avoid giving him those foods that you yourself shouldn't eat too heavily, like highly-seasoned food, fried foods, and too many potatoes.

Good grooming

If you keep your dog in the best possible condition at all times he will not only look his best but will feel his best too. Since the German Shepherd is a naturally sanitary dog, your problems will be small ones. All your grooming tasks will be easier if you make them fun for both you and the dog. Play with him and talk to him while you are brushing him, bathing him, or trimming his nails. Continually shouting and scolding your dog for not standing still will only make you irritable and the dog shy of grooming.

Since grooming can be pleasant and beneficial for both you and your pet, you should try to spend a few moments each day brushing him. Use a large metal comb on his coat first, then brush him vigorously with a wire brushing glove. Your pet shop sells both of these items, as well as all other grooming aids you will need. During the shedding seasons, in the spring and again in the fall, you will have to spend a little extra time getting loose hair from his coat. As you brush him, keep an eye peeled for any signs of skin disease or other disorders.

When you give your dog his daily brushing, check the length of his nails. If they are allowed to remain over-long they can cause lameness, spread toes, or foot diseases. You can get a special nail trimmer at your pet shop that will make the task easy. Cut off only the dead, horny part at the end of the nail. There is a tender part with a vein inside the nail called the "quick." Be careful not to cut the quick or you will cause your dog unnecessary pain. You can see the dark quick by holding your dog's paw near a strong light. After you have clipped off the ends of his nails, file off the sharp edges with a file of the type that a mechanic uses.

Only good health and good grooming will keep the good looks of a German Shepherd such as this.

The appropriate diet that is balanced by enough exercise will be sufficient in keeping your Shepherds lean and muscular.

Every few weeks you should check your Shepherd's teeth. If he has any broken or decayed ones, or shows any other unusual signs, you must get him to a veterinarian for care. Sometimes German Shepherds get tartar or discoloring on their teeth. If your dog has tartar deposits, take him to a veterinarian to have them cleaned. If his teeth are merely discolored, you can clean them with a special paste found in your local pet shop. An occasional treat of hard biscuit will help him clean his teeth himself.

If your dog's ears accumulate wax or dirt, clean them out with a cotton swab, being careful not to go in deep enough to hurt him. A commercially prepared medicated ear wash is available in most pet stores. Used as directed, this is quite helpful.

Bathing

Luckily for you, your German Shepherd does not require a bath too often. Use one of the detergents made especially for bathing dogs. Wash his head first, using a washcloth. Clean his ears thoroughly and be sure to dry them thoroughly afterwards. Be very careful not to get soapy water in his eyes or ears. After you have washed and rinsed his head, scrub his body thoroughly, then dry him with several large towels. Do not turn him loose until you are certain he is quite dry. He can easily catch cold by being out in the cool air with a damp coat. He will try to help you dry him by giving himself a good shaking and letting the water fly everywhere. This is one of those little problems that dog owners have that are really more fun than sorrow. If you cannot prevent it, you will just have to accept it; if you find a way to prevent it, please let other German Shepherd lovers know—they will appreciate being let in on the secret!

Giving first aid

Every dog owner is called upon at one time or another to give some form of first aid to his or someone else's pet. You may have to stop a hemorrhage, treat shock, or straighten and hold in place a broken leg. Remember that you should call the veterinarian in any case to follow up on your first aid; you should be prepared to give the proper treatment before the vet arrives.

Unless you have to, do not move the dog if there is a chance that he might have broken bones. When you have to move a strange dog, you should be sure to muzzle him. A small dog requires no more muzzling than a thick blanket folded about him. A larger dog, such as a German Shepherd, should probably be muzzled with one purchased at your local pet shop. Muzzling a dog this way gives you a chance to move him or handle him. Always be extremely careful when trying to muzzle a dog that's sick or in pain.

Illnesses

This section is intended to help you recognize some illnesses that your dog may get and help you to give temporary treatment in some cases. In any event, call a veterinarian. Only a person with years of training and experience can give your dog the care he needs when he is sick. Do not make the mistake of thinking that a helpful friend is a substitute for a veterinarian, no matter what illnesses your friend's dog may have recovered from.

Skin diseases: The skin diseases that dogs sometimes get are hard to tell apart, especially in the early stages. A veterinarian can, of course, diagnose them more easily. Be sure to continue applying medicine as long as the veterinarian says, even though it may look to you as

German Shepherds are not only intelligent and strong dogs but also affectionate and faithful—and they're dependable dogs for the home, too.

though the disease is cured. Sometimes the infection lingers just below the skin surface.

Mange is caused by tiny arthropods called "mites." They are not insects but are in the same family as spiders. The hair may fall out as it does in eczema, and the dog may scratch frantically at the infected area. Acne is the little red pimples and scales a puppy sometimes gets on his belly. Don't confuse this with flea bites. The cure for the latter is eliminating the fleas. It is not a serious disease. You can give temporary treatment by washing the belly with a little rubbing alcohol; then get your veterinarian's advice on further treatment. Often, itching and scratching can be the result of Sarcoptic Mange. A commercially prepared dog lotion to stop itching from this mange as well as other parasites and fungi is available in most pet shops. A further preventive is the use of a good flea and tick killer spray. Sometimes a skin disease can be contagious to humans. This is one of the few things transmissible from dog to man. So wash your hands carefully after handling a dog who shows skin lesions.

Distemper: Distemper is now, happily, a rather rare disease. It has not been completely eradicated, however, and is so serious that dog owners must be aware of it. A few of the signs of distemper are inflammation of the mucous membranes, discharges from the nose and eyes, nervousness, elevated temperature, diarrhea and possibly skin sores. Dogs can now be protected from distemper by immunizations, or "shots." One of the most important things you can do for your German Shepherd is to have a veterinarian give him these shots as early as possible.

Worms: There are many kinds of worms that may infest a dog. A few kinds are roundworms, hookworms and tapeworms. Some signs of worms are diarrhea and loss of appetite and weight, listlessness or a pot belly. Roundworms, which look like thin strands of spaghetti, can sometimes be seen in the feces or may be vomited up.

Most puppies get roundworms at one time or another. Fortunately, however, they are usually corrected by the addition of worm pills which are available at most pet shops. They can be fed to the puppy directly or added to his food. Tapeworms, which look like tan or pink grains of rice, may be seen in the feces or in the hair around the anal opening. Medicines are available for eliminating these. If, after treatment with these pills, the worms continue, it might be because of another type of worm. Whenever this condition persists, the dog should be taken to a veterinarian.

Cold or bronchitis: Only a veterinarian can distinguish with reasonable certainty between a common cold and bronchitis. Sore throat, tonsilitis, and pneumonia often show similar symptoms. Generally speaking, a dog will show signs about like those of a person with a cold. He will be listless and tired, may have a cough, and may have either diarrhea or constipation. If you cannot get your dog to a veterinarian immediately, keep him warm and quiet until the vet treats him.

Diarrhea and constipation: Diarrhea, sometimes called loose bowels, is usually caused by a change in diet or an intestinal disturbance. The dog may have to relieve himself eight or more times a day. The feces are watery and unformed. If there is no rise in temperature or other sign of illness, you may give the dog a tightening agent such as Kaopectate. If there is any blood in the feces or if the diarrhea persists for three or more days, call your veterinarian. If your dog becomes consti-

The picture of a German Shepherd in the best of health. Notice the intelligent and friendly expression, bright clear eyes, muscular and lean contours, and thick coat.

pated, his feces is hard and he must strain and grunt when relieving himself. Constipation is almost always caused by a faulty diet. You can give your dog immediate relief with commercially prepared products, then change his diet to one that promotes regularity. Add vegetables, fruit, and dog biscuits for ROUGHAGE and see that he gets plenty of water.

Fleas: Your dog will let you know immediately if he has fleas; he will scratch himself continually. For his general comfort, as well as to prevent him from catching any disease from the fleas, you should dust or bathe him to get rid of these little pests. Fleas also carry tapeworms. A flea collar will protect your pet against fleas and other external parasites for up to three months.

Heat strokes: NEVER leave your dog in a car that is sitting in the sun for any length of time. If you leave him in the car, be sure it is in the shade, that windows are open for ventilation, and that he has water to drink. If you ever have to treat a dog that has suffered a heat stroke, bathe him in cold water until his body temperature is lowered. If there is no tub handy, pour cold water over or rub his belly with a towel soaked in cold water and then take him to a vet immediately.

Call the vet

In giving first aid to your dog for any cause, remember to telephone the veterinarian as soon as possible. If you are in doubt about treatment, handle the dog's injury as you would that of a person.

Potential attackers will certainly think twice when they see a well trained German Shepherd. Photo by Sally Anne Thompson.

5.
Training

Housebreaking your puppy

Fortunately, the German Shepherd is such an intelligent dog that housebreaking him is not difficult. He soon senses what is required of him. For the first few weeks

Good behavior should be rewarded by kind words, a handshake, or a delectable tidbit. Photo by Sally Anne Thompson.

Jumping over obstacles for obedience training provides at the same time valuable exercise for your Shepherd. Photo by Sally Anne Thompson.

a young puppy may not understand your concern. Keep some newspapers on the floor in a corner and quickly carry the puppy to them when he cries or looks restless. If an accident occurs, do not rub his nose in it; this is cruel and accomplishes nothing. If you catch him in the act, shout "No" or "Shame" at him. If he does it on the newspapers, praise him lavishly and give him a "reward."

A commercially prepared housebreaking aid is available at most pet stores. This will aid in getting your dog to go to this one predetermined spot for this purpose.

When he is a few months old you should take him out after every meal and before bedtime. Praise him when he behaves and he will soon do what is required. If you walk him in the city be careful not to let him relieve himself on the sidewalk or on someone else's lawn.

Good manners

Good manners are just as important for dogs as for people. Every dog owner has the responsibility of training his dog to behave properly. It is not necessary for you to teach your dog any fancy tricks, but for the safety and welfare of the dog as well as that of yourself and others, you must teach him obedience to simple commands, such as "Come" and "Sit." The untrained dog brings a bad name to his owner and to his breed. One German Shepherd in your neighborhood who is a constant barker, or a nervous biter, will often cause people to hate all German Shepherds, good or bad.

Swimming can be highly therapeutic for older dogs with a slight hip problem. Photo by Sally Anne Thompson.

This German Shepherd has learned to stay "down." He keeps his position without regard to the trainer stepping over him. Photo by Sally Anne Thompson.

German Shepherds, being intelligent and alert, are easy to train if you follow a few basic rules: (1) Be firm and consistent. Use the same commands for each lesson, and use the dog's name before each command. (2) Be patient. Your German Shepherd is intelligent but he can't talk your language. When you lose your patience and begin shouting at the dog you will only confuse him. (3) Reward him with kind words and petting. He needs and wants your love during training. (4) Keep the lessons short... Ten or fifteen minutes at a time is plenty.

The retrieval of objects is a normal behavior of dogs, but doing it on command requires training.

This picture illustrates the power and strength of a German Shepherd. Photo by Sally Anne Thompson.

You will need a collar and a leash for training your dog. There are many types available and your pet shop salesman will be happy to help you select one. Allow the dog to wear the new collar for several days before training begins so that he may become accustomed to it.

You should first teach your dog to walk at your side, and always on the left side. Simply walk along with your dog at your side until he moves in a different direction than the one in which you want to go. Then stop and hold the leash firmly until he comes back to your side. Then walk on again until he strays from the right direction. Again, stop and wait for him to return. No verbal commands are necessary. He wants to be able to walk and he soon learns that the only way he will get to keep moving is by staying at your side.

You can teach your dog to come at command by the following method. Allow him to go to the end of a long leash, then call him to you by saying his name and "Come" or "Here." If he does not immediately come to your side, pull the leash gently until he does. Get him to you even if you have to drag him part of the way. Reward him with kind words and petting when he reaches you.

If you allow your dog to jump up on you with his front paws, you will soon lose most of your friends and gain a cleaning and laundry bill that only a millionaire could afford. When he first does this, grab his front legs and hold them firmly in a high position. Keep him in this position for ten or twenty seconds. The dog finds this uncomfortable and should soon stop jumping on you. If he persists, tramp on his hind paws while you hold his

Learning how to stay "down" correctly and comfortably.

front legs up; this is practically guaranteed to teach him. A larger dog can be broken by raising your knee as he rears up. Bumping his soft underparts against your hard knee is a good deterrent.

Since German Shepherds do grow so large and can leave a lot of hair on furniture, you will probably want to train your dog to stay off the furniture. If you catch him in the act, shout "No" or "Shame" at him, and push him off the furniture if necessary. If he sneaks onto the couch when you are not around, other methods become

For security, be sure your fence is sufficiently high for a good jumper such as your German Shepherd. Photo by A. Winzell.

Choose the appropriate size and equipment for the formal training of your Shepherd. Such equipment should be well constructed and made of durable and safe material.

necessary. A commercially prepared preparation can help keep dogs off special pieces of furniture or carpeting.

A word of caution. The German Shepherd has been developed as a guard dog. His natural tendency is to protect. It is very cute to see a little puppy bark and growl at strangers, but if he is encouraged to do this he may turn vicious. Allow him to bark for a minute or so and then tell him firmly "Quiet" at the same time holding his mouth closed with your hand. Repeat this until he learns the command. When he rushes aggressively at people quickly command "Sit" and if he is well trained he will obey automatically. Pet him until he calms down. Don't worry. He'll still protect you with his life should the occasion arise; however, proper training will help protect the innocent visitors. It is very uncomfortable for someone to sit in a room with a large dog which keeps growling at him, glaring balefully and leaping up at every movement. Be considerate of your guests and discipline your pet beforehand.

The male is much more aggressive than the female, so for a family dog the female is usually a better choice. She is easier to housebreak and train.

The aforementioned aggressive tendencies often do not manifest themselves until the dog is a year or two old. At this age he is extremely powerful so it is best to instill the habit of obedience in him while he is still a puppy.

For further training you may wish to enter your dog in obedience classes. Your pet shop owner will know of classes being held in your area and will be glad to help you.

6.
Breeding

Pride and mating

If you have a good female German Shepherd that you are proud of, you may wish to breed her. You may plan to keep the puppies as pets, sell them, or even (if you

Breeding as close as possible to an "ideal" German Shepherd is the goal of a serious breeder of this popular breed. Photo by Sally Anne Thompson.

are lucky in the litter) show some of them. Whatever your plans, you should consider all aspects carefully before you breed your German Shepherd. There are any number of good books on breeding dogs in general and German Shepherds in particular. Your pet shop can recommend one for you.

Types of breeding

Three types of dog breeding are practiced. *Inbreeding* is the mating of dogs that are closely related. If you mate brother and sister, parent to offspring, or cousin to cousin, you are inbreeding. Rigid selection should be employed because inbreeding doubles up family traits.

These German Shepherds are bred for conformation, hence they are expected to represent qualities close to the standard of the breed. Photo by Louise van der Meid.

Be cautious of handling very young puppies. The mother German Shepherd is especially protective at this stage.

Your Shepherd must learn how to "sit" as early as possible. Sitting is a natural stance and quite easy to learn. Photo by Sally Anne Thompson.

While the good traits of the family are brought out, so are the bad. Inbreeding brings about a higher chance of recessive characteristics showing up in the litter. Inbreeding is often used with excellent results.

Linebreeding, the breeding of dogs who are distant relatives, and *outbreeding*, the mating of unrelated or very distantly related dogs, is more commonly done. Set your goal in terms of what you wish to accomplish: a desired characteristic, a particular color, or a certain temperament. Choose the sire which you think will best bring this about.

In brief, each characteristic your dog possesses is determined by the genes which he inherits from his parents.

The female German Shepherd that is bred is called a brood bitch. A bitch is first capable of having puppies when she is about eight to twelve months old. Most breeders prefer to wait about six months longer when she comes into her next season to bear puppies.

If you want the best-looking puppies that you can get, you must choose your female's mate, or stud dog, carefully. Breeding to a highly rated stud dog can cost as much as several hundred dollars. Sometimes the owner of the stud will take a "pick of the litter," his choice of a puppy, in part payment of the stud fee. You will want to investigate the backgrounds of the available stud dogs and get as many opinions from experienced breeders as possible. Your female should be in the best possible health before breeding. This is good insurance that the puppies will be healthy. After she has been bred, pay special attention to her diet so that she gets all the vitamins and minerals she needs. Do not let her exercise too vigorously, she may injure herself or the puppies.

The puppies should be delivered nine weeks from the day she was bred, though delivery may vary a day or two either way. Arrange to purchase a bed from your local pet shop especially for this purpose. Place the bed in a very quiet, warm area for her sometime before the puppies are due, and get her accustomed to using it. She will handle the birthing of the puppies herself, delivering them one at a time and cleaning them. It is unlikely that she will need help, but you should stand by just in case. If this is her first litter, you may wish to have someone a little more expert, perhaps the owner of the stud dog, on hand with you.

The gestation period is from 59 to 63 days. During this period leave your bitch alone as much as possible. Don't fuss over her. During the first few weeks you may worm or bathe her if necessary. You may also wish to give her inoculations for distemper and hepatitis to increase the pups' immunity when they are born. She will probably be very uncomfortable during the last weeks of her pregnancy. Restrain her activities, and if she loses her appetite tempt her with the foods she likes.

Birthing

Watch for the first sign of labor pain; she will pant, strain and stretch her body. Note the time. If all is going well, within an hour you will see a lump between anus and vulva. (If she is in labor more than one hour without producing a pup, call the veterinarian.) Then, after a few more strainings, a thin opaque fluid-filled sac will appear. She will probably expel it without assistance. If she needs help, use a terry cloth washrag to get a grip on its slick surface and, with each succeeding labor strain, pull down gently but firmly. The bitch will usually rip the sac open with her teeth and chew the umbilical cord which will later dry up and break off.

The pups will continue to arrive, perhaps half an hour apart; perhaps a full hour or more. The same labor strainings will accompany each. You can usually tell when the final pup has been born: the mother will relax and seem to sigh in contentment.

The cute little puppies

After the puppies are born, keep plenty of newspapers on the floor in their area for housebreaking purposes. Avoid the temptation to show the cute little puppies to your friends for the first week. Like any good mother, the female German Shepherd does not like a lot of strangers handling her babies and she will be nervous. This will pass in a week or two, though, and you may show your new pets to your friends.

At about three weeks you will want to start weaning the puppies. The dewclaws—tiny extra claws growing on the inside of the dog's legs—should be removed by the vet when the pups are no more than a week old. (While visiting him for this, make appointments for the puppies' inoculations.) The eyes will open at nine or ten days after birth.

German Shepherds' looks are to a good extent dependent on hereditary factors—but the environment you provide for your pet counts a lot also.

German Shepherds are devoted parents. Photo by Isabelle Francaise. Courtesy of E. Martin (Highland Hills German Shepherds) and J. McDonnell.

7.
Showing

After you have spent a year with your German Shepherd you will probably feel that he is the greatest dog in the world. If, in addition, you have opinions from breeders or others who know show dogs, that yours has good

An outdoor dog show held in England. Photo by Sally Anne Thompson.

Strong rich colors are preferred in German Shepherds, faded or pale ones are faulted, and white is completely disallowed.

"points" or show features, you will undoubtedly want to enter him in shows.

The best ally you can have in this endeavor is an experienced handler. There are many little things you will have to learn about training your Shepherd for shows, grooming him properly, and handling him to the best advantage. German Shepherd breeders and handlers are enthusiastic about the breed. They are always happy, even anxious, to let you in on their "secrets" of showing. You can, of course, get much of this information from books, and you should read before showing your dog.

Before showing your German Shepherd, compare him against the standards of the breed. Enter him first in a local show to see what the judges think of him; if he does well, it is then time to consider a major show. But before deciding to show your dog at all, consider your motives. Do not enter if you cannot accept losing. Remember that if your dog does not win, it does not mean that he is an inferior dog. He is just as wonderful as he always was! In short, ask yourself what the outcome of a show would mean in terms of your attitude toward him. If you think it would alter your affection, forget the whole idea.

Familiarize yourself with a major dog show as a spectator before you actually enter your German Shepherd. Have a clear understanding of what is expected of you and your dog. If you do not believe your dog is ready for a major show, you may prefer to hire a professional to help you prepare him.

Consult the various dog magazines to discover the dates of coming shows. Decide which you would like to enter and write to the show secretary requesting the "premium list" and entry forms. You will be required to pay an entry fee. There are five major classifications in which your German Shepherd may be entered:

Puppy Class: Six to twelve-month-old puppies whelped in the United States or Canada.

Novice Class: Dogs six months or older who have not won a first prize except in a puppy class. Again these dogs must have been whelped in the United States or Canada.

Exhibitor Class: Dogs who are more than six months old, who are not champions but who are exhibited by recognized breeders.

American Bred Class: Dogs who are not champions, who are whelped in the United States from a mating which took place in the United States.

Open Class: Any dog six months of age or more may enter here.

You can almost see the pride in her puppies shining from the eyes of this proud German Shepherd mother.

8.
Guarding

Born to working, your German Shepherd displays both intelligence and beauty. He is the automatic guardian of your home and your most faithful friend.

Though called the "Police Dog" or "Seeing-Eye Dog"

Not all German Shepherds qualify for training as "seeing-eye dogs." Note the special harness for this type of work. Photo by Sally Anne Thompson.

Examine the teeth of your Shepherd regularly. Small abnormalities must be attended to before they develop into serious conditions.

because of his accomplishments in those fields, the German Shepherd has become the canine prototype of leader and guardian. He has the capacity to learn, one of the reasons he's chosen to guide the blind. "Seeing-Eye" schools "educate" rather than train, for their animals must do more than exhibit a reflex to commands. They must think, and the German Shepherd is one of the few breeds that can consistently turn out to be *"cum laude"* graduates.

To bark or not to bark

Most young dogs will bark at anything and everybody; a few are so friendly that they will not. Highly important in training a watchdog is to teach him when to, and when not to bark. Teaching him when not to bark will save you from annoyance; teaching him when to bark will protect you from intruders.

A dog that barks incessantly is not an effective watchdog. When he barks he should always know that you will come and investigate. At the beginning he may consider every sound a threat. He will not be able to distinguish between friend and foe. He will even bark at grandma when she comes to visit. It will take weeks of patient training before he will be able to sort out all these various sounds and people and decide which are to be barked at. If he is to be a good watchdog, it is far better for him to bark at everyone and everything until you have commanded him to be quiet.

There has to be a happy medium somewhere in a dog's barking, or not barking. If yours is to be a guard dog it is probably better to encourage barking rather than to discourage it.

Refusing food from strangers

To be effective as a watchdog, your dog must be taught never to accept food or water from strangers. This will keep him safe from any poisoned or doped food which a would-be intruder might offer him.

Always feed your dog in the same spot and in the same bowl. If at all possible, always let the same person do the feeding. Make sure, of course, that he is fed enough.

Owners soon discover that the German Shepherd learns rapidly. Training becomes a pleasure. This dog doesn't forget lessons! Often, he seems to learn by himself. He becomes a member of the family, not only in acceptance, but in duties and responsibilities. He measures up to your expectations—and maybe even more. To millions, he is THE DOG. He looks like what a dog should look like, but his actions and thinking appear human. The German Shepherd deserves all the popularity and praise he receives. He adds to the stature of his master, and rewards him with affection and love.